Tourism
&
Airline Service
English

한올출판사

Contents

Part 1 | Airline Service English

Contents

Part 2 | Tourism Service English

Part 3 | 부 록

PART 1

Airline Service English

CHAPTER 1 Ticketing & boarding

Dialogue 1

A : Agent T : Tourist

A : Good Morning, Sir. How may I help you?

T : I'd like to buy a ticket to New York.

A : Would you like to buy a one-way or round-trip ticket?

T : A round trip ticket, please.

A : When would you like to leave?

T : On September 9th.

A : Economy or business class, sir?

T : Business class, please.

A : Do you have seating preference?

T : If possible, I'd like a window seat.

A : Ok, sir. Your flight number is 503 to New York leaving at 10 a.m. Please proceed to gate 19 at 9:30 a.m.

T : Thank you.

Dialogue 2

A : Agent P : Passenger

T : Hello, is this Asiana Air ticketing counter?

A : Yes, it is.

T : I already have a reservation. So, I would like to buy my ticket.

A : May I have your name?

T : Charles.

A : Your flight number is KE 707 to New York, business class, right?

T : Yes, How much do I pay for it?

A : It's 500 dollars.
Do you have any baggage to check?

T : Yes, I have two suitcases.

A : O.K. How would you like to pay?

T : Do you accept traveler's checks?

A : Sure.

T : Here it is.

A : Thank you. Have a nice trip.

Dialogue 3

A : Agent T : Tourist

A : Could you show me your ticket and passport, please?

T : Here you are.

A : Are you going to London via Japan by British Airways 345, economy class?

T : That's right.

A : Would you prefer an aisle seat or a window seat?

T : A window seat, please.

A : All right. Here are your boarding pass, passport and ticket.
Your boarding time is 9:00a.m. at gate 3. You should be there 20 minutes prior to departure.

T : Thank you.

Dialogue 4

T : Tourist A : Agent

A : I'am sorry, sir. The flight is over booked and we can't allow some passengers to board.

T : What are you talking about? I already have a confirmed reservation and a valid ticket.

A : Of course I know, but unfortunately it is impossible for you to board this flight now. All I can do for you is to book alternate flight arrangements.

T : Ok. then, when is the next flight?

A : Well, our next flight to Alaska is at 6 in the evening. There are some seats available on the flight. Would you mind accepting this new schedule?

T : No, I have no choice.

A : Ok. Wait a moment, please.

....

Thank you. Here is your new boarding pass.

We've upgraded your seat as a compensation.

T : I see, thank you anyway.

A : We are sorry you missed your flight.

T : That's ok.

A : Thank you. Enjoy your trip.

Air Service English Vocabulary

- Take–off 이륙
- Accompanied Baggage 휴대수하물
- Accuracy 정확도
- Acknowledge 응답하다
- Acrobatic 곡예비행
- Actual time of Arrival(ATA) 실제도착시간
- Actuator 작동장치
- Additional Equipment 추가장비
- Advanced Technology 첨단기술
- Aerodrome Control Service 비행장 관제업무
- Elevation 고도, 해발
- Air Cargo 항공화물
- Air Carrier 항공운송회사
- Air Current 기류
- Air Evacuation 항공우송
- Air Mail 항공우편
- Air Express 항공배달서비스
- Air Fare 항공요금
- Air Field 비행장

- Air Pressure 기압
- Air Route 항로
- Air Sickness 비행기멀미
- Air Ticket 비행기표
- Air Traffic Control 항공교통관제(탑)
- Air Way 항로
- Airborne Radar 기상레이더
- Aircraft Equipment 항공장비
- Airflow 기류
- Airline 항공로
- Airlines 항공사
- Airport 공항
- Aisle seat 통로좌석 예 Window seat 창가좌석
- Atmosphere 대기권

Interview Basic Questions

※ **Answer the following questions briefly.**

1. How do you feel today?

2. What date is it today?
   What day is it today?

3. How do you get here?
   How long did it take?

4. What salary do you expect?

5. Please tell me about your physical status, height, weight, eyesight.
   (Can you tell me about yourself?)

Situation English Tips

1. Question about flight. (trip)

Q : How was the flight (trip)

Q : Was the trip all right?

Q : Did you have a good flight?

A : (긍정)

Yes,	it was very good. quite good. Not too bad.	Thanks.

A : (부정)

No,	not very good. rather tiring (very tiring). a bit rough.

2. Question about Weather.

Q : 좋은 날씨

It is	nice and warm hot sunny mild beautiful	today	isn't it?
	lovely day		

Answer 1

Yes,	It is	very nice beautiful wonderful

Answer 2

Yes,	It is	horrible dreadful terrible awful

Translation

NO	Korean sentence	English sentence
School life		
1	승무원이 되기 위해 항공서비스학과에 입학하였습니다.	To become a flight attendant, I entered the Airline Service Department.
2	제 전공은 경력에 많은 도움이 될 최고의 선택입니다.	My major is one of the best decisions on my life and will be helpful in my career.
3	학생회를 이끌면서 리더십을 배우고 책임감을 향상시킬 수 있었습니다.	Leading the student body taught me a lot about leadership, and it helped me to develop a sense of responsibility, too.
4	제 전공은 제 분야에서 전문가로 성장하도록 도와주었고 자신감과 자긍심을 심어주었습니다.	My major has helped me grow as a professional in my field and gave me the confidence and pride I carry today.
5	다른 학생들과 잘 어울리며 그들의 의견을 항상 경청하려고 합니다.	I get along well with the other students and always try to listen to their opinions.

CHAPTER 2

Inflight Service(I)

Dialogue 1

F : Flight Attendant P : Passenger

P : Excuse me, my friend and I were assigned separate seats.
Do you have any vacant seats so that we can sit together?

F : I'll see if it can be arranged. I'll come back and let you know, sir.

P : O.K. Thanks.

....

F : Thank you for your waiting, sir.
We have some seats in the back of the cabin. Would it be alright?

P : That's fine, Thank you.

F : May I help you with your bags?

P : No, thank you. That's all right.

F : Please come this way. Here are your seats.

Have a good flight!

Dialogue 2

F : Flight Attendant P : Passenger

P : Excuse me, but there is someone in my seat.

F : May I see your boarding pass, please?

Let me check on that. Perhaps there has been a mistake in seating arrangements. Would you mind waiting here, ma'am?

I'll get back to you soon.

P : O.K.

F : Thank you for waiting, ma'am.

Your seat is 55h. I'm sorry for the inconvenience.

P : That's o.k.

F : I'll show you where it is.

This way, please.

Here is your seat.

P : Thank you for your help.

F : Would you like something to drink?

P : No, thank you.

Dialogue 3

F : Flight Attendant P : Passenger

P : Do you have any window seats available?

F : Would you wait until everyone is on board? Let me check after that, ma'am.

P : O.k.

F : We just have a window seat left in the middle of the cabin. Would you like to change?

P : Oh, yes, that would be fine.

F : This way, please. Here is your seat.
By the way, may I put your bag in the overhead bin for you?

P : No, thank you.
I'll keep my bag under my seat.

F : O.k. Is there anything else I can do for you?

P : No, that is o.k.

F : Enjoy your flight, ma'am.

Dialogue 4

F : Flight Attendant P : Passenger

F : Excuse me, sir. Would you mind fastening your seatbelt, please?

P : Oh, I see, By the way, would you show me how to fasten it?

F : Certainly sir, just insert this part of the belt into the buckle.

P : I see. Before that, can I use the restroom now?

F : Yes, but please hurry. We will be taking off soon.

P : Thank you. When do we take-off?

F : In about 15 minutes, we will take off, sir.

P : Then how long does it take to get to Alaska?

F : About 7 hours.

P : I see. Thank you.

Air Service English Vocabulary

- Baby Bassinet 기내용 유아요람
- Baggage 짐, 수하물
- Barrier 방벽, 울타리
- Beverage 음료
- Boarding pass 탑승권
- Boarding Time 탑승시간
- Cancellation 결항(항공편의)
- Captain 기장
- Cargo Aircraft 화물기
- Cargo Warehouse 화물창고
- Catering Service 식음료 서비스
- Check-in 탑승수속
- Claim Check 위탁수하물
- Clearance 통관수속, 입국허가, 비행허가
- Confirm 예약을 확인하다.
- Reconfirm 예약을 재확인하다.
- Customs Declaration Form 세관신고서
- Customs Duty 관세
- Customs Inspection 세관심사
- Customs Inspector 세관심사원

Interview Basic Questions

※ **Answer the following questions briefly.**

1. What's the weather today?

2. Can you tell me about your personality?

3. What kind of man(woman) do you like?

4. Can you describe one of your best friends?

5. How many members are there in your family?

6. What is your merit?

7. What is your weakpoint?

Situation English Tips

Is	this seat taken / occupied? your sister married?	Yes, it is. / No, it isn't. Yes, she is. / No, she isn't.
Was	it cold this afternoon? she angry with you?	Yes, it was. No, she wasn't.

Are there	any countries to visit? any questions to ask?	Yes, there are. No, there aren't.
Is there	a duty-free shop near here? a city-hall near here? anyone you know?	Yes, there is. No, there isn't. No, there isn't.

Have you	ever been to America? filled out this reservation form?	Yes, I have. No, I haven't.
Has	she arrived in Seoul? it stopped raining?	Yes, she has. No, it hasn't.

Do (Can)	you live in Seoul? you speak English?	Yes, I do. No, I can't.
Does Did	this bag belong to you? you see her last night?	Yes, it does. No, I didn't.

Translation

1	저는 항공서비스학과를 전공해서 저의 전공지식을 활용할 수 있는 직업을 갖고 싶습니다.	I majored in Airline Service. So I want a job where I can use my major.
2	장학금을 받은 것이 제 최고의 성과였다고 여겨집니다.	One of my best achievements is probably when I was awarded a scholarship.
3	대학생활의 삶과 다양한 친구를 사귀게 된 것이 제 삶에 큰 영향을 주었습니다.	Living on campus and having friends with different backgrounds has been a big influence on my life.
4	우리 대학은 직업중심의 교육으로 유명합니다.	Our university is well-known for the career-oriented contents of its courses.
5	제 적성과 잘 맞는 전공이라서 기쁩니다.	I'm happy with my major because it is a perfect fit for my aptitude.

Inflight Service(Ⅱ)

CHAPTER 3

Dialogue 1

F : Flight Attendant P : Passenger

F : Good afternoon, sir? Would you care for something to drink?
We have juice, soft drinks, water, and beer.

P : Orange juice, please. And what kind of beer do you have?

F : We have Budweiser and Hite.

P : I'd like a Budweiser.

F : Here you are. Anyting else?

P : Could I have another drink, please?

F : Sure. What would you like?

P : I'll have a scotch, please.

F : How would you like your scotch?

P : Straight, please. And peanuts, too.

F : O.k. wait a minute, please.

.... Here is your drink for you............. May I take away your glass?

P : Yes, please. I'm finished.

Dialogue 2

F : Flight Attendant　　　　P : Passenger

F : Good afternoon, ma'am. We'll be serving meals now. May I set up your tray table?

P : Sure. What's the meal today?

F : We have beef and fish for lunch. Which one would you prefer?

P : I will have beef, please. I am allergic to seafood.

F : Here's your meal. ..... Have you finished with your meal?

P : Yes.

F : May I take your meal tray?

P : Yes, Please.

F : Would you like something to drink?

P : I'll have some coffee.

F : Do you need cream and sugar?

P : Yes, I do.

Dialogue 3

F : Flight Attendant P : Passenger

P : Excuse me, I requested a vegetarian meal when I made a reservation.

F : I am sorry, sir. May I have your name, please?

P : Robert Brown.

F : Wait a moment, please. Let me check on your meal right away.

....

Sir, I am very sorry, it was not loaded. May I offer you another meal?

P : Well then, can you give me some bread and salad instead?

F : Alright. I'll get it for you right away. … Thank you for waiting. Here's your meal. Please accept our apologies.

Is there anything else I can do for you?

P : Yes, I have a headache. Do you have anything for that?

F : I'll bring some Asprine right away. … Here you are. Please take two tablets at one time. I hope you feel better.

P : Thank you.

Dialogue 4

F : Flight Attendant P : Passenger

P : Excuse me. what kind of duty free items can I get here?

F : Please look over the duty free goods magazine in the seat pocket.
Would you like to order any duty free goods?

P : Yes, do you have perfume and liquor?

F : Of course. What kind of perfume would you like?
We have 'Channel No.5', 'Polo', and 'Christian Dior'. And We have many kinds of liquor. Johnnie Walker, Chivas Regal, Camus and some Scotch Whisky.

P : I want 'Channel No.5' and a bottle of Johnnie Walker, please.
Can I pay in korean won?

F : Yes, you can.

Air Service English Vocabulary

- Date of Issue 발권일자
- Declaration 세관신고 declare 신고하다.
- Departure 출발
- Deposit 예치금
- Ditching 비상착륙
- Domestic Airport 국내선 전용공항
- Duration 여행기간
- Duty Free Goods 면세품
- Duty Free Shop 면세점
- Emergency(Exit) 비상구, 비상사태
- Export 수출
- Extension 체류연장, 구내전화
- Fare 운임
- Farewell 작별
- Fasten Seat Belt 안전벨트 매다
- Fatigue 피로
- First Aid 응급처치, 비상약
- First class 일등석
- Flight Deck 조종실
- Forced Landing 비상착륙

Interview Basic Questions

※ **Answer the following questions briefly.**

1. What is your major?
   What did you learn from your major?

2. What is the most memorable thing in your campus life?

3. Can you tell me about your working experience?

4. If you become a flight attendant, what kind of service would you like to offer?

Situation English Tips

How	do you know him? many members are in your family? much money do you get paid? long does it take? large is in your class?
When	do you usually study English? did you visit korea? can you see the girl?
Where	do you live? did you go yesterday?
Which	country are you from? book do you like to read?
Why	do you want this job? are you late? did you say like that?
Could Would May	you tell me what you like? you mind telling me your phone number? I ask your name?

Translation

NO	Korean sentence	English sentence
	Strong Points	
1	저의 장점은 조직력이 뛰어나다는 점입니다.	My strength is that I have good organizational skills.
2	저는 체계적으로 일하고 다른 사람과 의시소통히는데 능숙합니다.	I am good at organizing and communicating with others.
3	의사결정을 신속하게 할 수 있습니다.	I am able to make quick decisions.
4	저는 효율적으로 여러 가지 일을 동시에 할 수 있는 사람입니다.	I am an efficient multi-tasker.
5	저는 스트레스가 되는 환경에서도 일을 할 수 있습니다.	I am able to work under stress.
6	스트레스가 되는 상황에서도 침착성을 유지하려고 노력합니다.	I try to stay calm even under stressful circumstances.
7	적응이 빨라서 일을 빨리 배웁니다.	My adaptability allows me to be a fast learner.

CHAPTER 4

InFlight Announcement Ⅰ

Announcement 1

(Boarding pass checking and baggage securing)

Ladies and gentleman,

This is Asiana Airline flight No.707 bound for New York.

Please check your flight number.

The use of electronic devices such as mobile phones is not allowed at any time during the flight.

Please turn off your mobile phone and other electronic devices.

And so, for your comfort and safety please keep all carry-on baggage in the overhead bins or under the seat in front of you. When you open the overhead compartments, please be careful as the contents may fall out.

For more information, please refer to the 'Hight Life' magazine in your seat pocket.

Thank you for your cooperation.

Announcement 2

(welcome)

Good afternoon, ladies and gentlemen.

Captain Jeong and the entire crew would like to welcome you aboard on Asiana Airline flight 707.

Our flight time will be 7hours 30minutes.

Please make sure your seat belt is securely fastened.

And please return your seat back and tray table to the upright position.

The use of electronic devices including mobile phones is not allowed during taking off and landing.

Smoking in the cabin and lavatories is prohibited at all times during the flight.

We're pleased to have you on board today and we'll do our best to serve you.

Thank you.

Announcement 3

(Safty Demonstration)

Ladies and gentlemen, this is the passenger safety briefing of this aircraft.

In case of an emergency evacuation, please follow the illuminated emergency lights in the cabin.

Passengers seated in an emergency exit row will be required to assist other passengers' evacuation following the instructions of our cabin crew.

To fasten the seat belt, insert the metal tong into the buckle and pull the loose end for tightening. To release the seat belt, lift up the metal cover.

In case of a cabin decompression, oxygen masks will drop automatically.

Pull the mask toward you and cover your nose and mouth with the mask, then adjust the head band.

Life vests are stowed under your seat for emergency ditching.

To put the vest on, slip it over your head, take the strap and put it around your waist, then fasten. Tighten your vest by pulling down on the strap.

To inflate the vest, pull down on the red tabs.

Additional air can be supplied into the vest by blowing into the tubes on each side of the vest.

Inflate the vest just before you are ready to exit the aircraft.

For more information, please review the passenger safety briefing card.

Thank you.

Announcement 4

(Seat belt sign off)

Ladies and gentlemen

Although the seat belt sign has been turned off, in case of sudden turbulence,

Please keep your seat belt fastened at all times during the flight.

We'd like to remind you that smoking is not allowed in the cabin and lavatories.

Your cooperation is much appreciated.

Thank you.

Air Service English Vocabulary

- Gauge 계기, 게이지
- Generator 발전기
- Ground staff 지상근무요원
- Gust 돌풍
- Hail 우박
- Hand Carried Baggage 기내에 가지고 들어갈 수 있는 짐 가방
- Heat Treatment 열처리
- Heavy oil 중유
- Heavy snow warning 폭설경보
- Height 높이
- Holding area 대기구역
- Hovering 제자리비행
- Humidity 습도
- Infant Fare 유아운임
- Inflight Announcement 기내안내방송
- Inflight Duty-free sale 기내 면세품판매
- Inspection 통관심사
- Inspector 검사관

- International Airport 국제공항
- Interpreter 통역

Interview Basic Questions

※ **Answer the following questions briefly.**

1. Why do you think you are qualified for this position?

2. How do you behave in case of emergency during the flight?

3. Have you applied for any other airlines?

4. How long do you want to work as a flight attendant?

5. Which one is more important : Safety or good service?

Situation English Tips

1. Suggestion 1

	shall we	drink?
	would you like to	
What	do you suggest we	have/ eat?
	do you want to	do tonight?
	can we	

2. Time expression

this coming Sunday	the day before yesterday
this summer	the day after tomorrow
this evening	this weekend

3. Suggestion 2

What(How) about Do you feel like	going to the movies?
Shall we Let's Why don't we Why not	go to the park? take a walk?
Answer	That's a good idea. That's would be nice.

Translation

1	저는 어떤 경우에도 절대 지각하지 않습니다.	I never show up late.
2	저는 침착한 사람으로 평정을 잃지 않습니다.	I am a calm person and never lose my temper.
3	착하고 성실하다는 애기를 많이 들었습니다.	People have often told me that I am nice and hard-working.
4	저는 대인관계가 능숙합니다.	I have good interpersonal skills.
5	저는 목표중심적이고 책임감이 있습니다.	I am quite a goal-oriented and responsible person.
6	다양한 사람을 응대할 수 있는 것이 저의 큰 장점 중에 하나입니다.	One of my biggest strengths is that I have the ability to deal with all types of people.
7	저는 열정적이고 열린 마음을 가지고 있으며 의사소통능력이 뛰어납니다.	I am an enthusiastic and openminded person who has excellent communication skills.
8	저의 장점은 매사에 긍정적이고 무슨 일이든 최선을 다합니다.	My strong point is that I do my best in everything with a positive attitude.

InFlight Announcement Ⅱ

CHAPTER 5

Announcement 1

(Service Plan)

Ladies and gentleman

This is your captain, speaking.
We apologize for the delay in our departure.
And I would like to inform you of our service flow for this flight. We will be serving cocktails and soft drinks followed by lunch soon.

Following the meal service, duty free items will be offered in all cabins. Then we will be presenting movies and a selection of short films. We will also serve breakfast before landing.

For further details on service procedures refer to your sky magazine in your seat pocket. If you need any assistance, please let us know.
We are at your entire service throughout the flight to make your trip a pleasant one.

Thank you.

Announcement 2

(duty–free sales)

Ladies and gentlemen

In a few minutes, we'll begin our sales of duty–free items.

If you'd like to purchase any items, please let us know.
Full details of our selection of liquors, cigarettes, perfumes and other items are give in the inflight magazine which you will find in the seat pocket in front of you.

We accept Korean won, U.S dollar, Japanese yen and credit card.

For your convenience, we have a pre–order form which will allow you to order items and pick them up on your return flight.

For further information, please contact your flight attendants.

Thank you.

Announcement 3

(movie and headphone collection)

Ladies and gentlemen

We shall shortly begin our feature film which we hope you will enjoy watching. Today's film is entitled '○○○○○○○○○', a romantic drama starring ○○○ and ○○○. Headsets are obtainable from the cabin crew, and the English soundtrack of '○○○○○○○○○' is channel 10 for the first class cabin and channel 20 for economy class. Music is available on the other channels and details are given in the inflight magazine, which may be found in the pocket of the seat in front of you.

Ladies and gentlemen,

We hope you have enjoyed our entertainment program. Our flight attendants will collect your headphones shortly.

Your cooperation is much appeciated.

Thank you.

Announcement 4

(Landing)

Ladies and gentlemen

We've just landed at London Airport.

The local time in London is 10 a.m. For your safety, please remain seated with your seatbelt fastened, until we come to a complete stop and the Captain turns off the seat belt sign. Please be sure to take all of your belongings with you when you exit.

And be careful when opening the overhead compartments, since bags may have shifted during the flight.

....

You may now exit through the forward door and please make sure to take all of your belongings with you when you exit.

On behalf of the entire flight crew, we would like to express our sincere thanks to all of you for flying British Airways. We look forward to serving you again in the near future.

We wish you a pleasant stay in London.

Good bye.

Air Service English Vocabulary

- Jet Blast 제트분사
- Jet Liner 제트여객기
- Jet Stream 제트기류
- Junior Crew 신입승무원
- Key Item 주요품목
- Kite 연
- Landing 착륙
- Landing Speed 착륙속도
- Launch 발사
- Launch Deck 발사대
- Layout 배회, 배열
- Lead Time 소요시간
- Level Flight 수평비행
- Life Jacket(Vest) 구명조끼
- Lift 양력
- Liquid Fuel 액체연료
- Local Time 현지시간
- Lock 잠금
- Lost and Found 유실물 취급소
- Low-rate 낮은 요금

Interview Basic Questions

※ **Answer the following questions briefly.**

1. Can you speak English well?

2. What is the disadvantage or advantage of working as a flight attendant?

3. Have you ever studied abroad?

4. How have you studied English?

5. Can you speak any other foreign language except English?

Situation English Tips

Likes and Dislikes

I	like enjoy love	reading books. cooking. going camping.
I am	fond of	dancing. jogging.
Answer	Do you?	me, too. so do I.
	Are you?	I am not. I don't like at all.
		That's incredible.

I	don't like dislike hate	Watching TV. the cold. Junk food. humid weather.
Answer	Neither do I. I don't like it, either.	

Translation

NO	Korean sentence	English sentence
	Personality traits	
1	이해심이 많고 신뢰가 간다는 애기를 친구들한테서 많이 듣는 편입니다.	My friends often tell me that I am understanding and trust-worthy.
2	저는 언변도 능하지만 다른 사람의 말을 잘 경청합니다.	I am a good talker and listener.
3	저는 자발적으로 계획을 실행하는 편입니다.	I'm very self-motivated.
4	저는 항상 시간을 엄수합니다.	I am punctual.
5	저는 융통성 있고 느긋한 편입니다.	I'm flexible and easygoing
6	저는 사람들과 어울리는 것을 좋아합니다.	I am fond of getting along with people.
7	제가 하는 일은 즐겁게 하는 성격입니다.	I am a person who enjoys what I do.
8	저는 자기계발을 위해 많은 것들을 합니다.	I do many things to develop myself.

CHAPTER 6

Handling Customer's Requests

Dialogue 1

F : Flight Attendant P : Passenger

F : Please return your seat to the upright position. And open your tray table, please.

P : Sure.

F : Here is your meal, sir.

P : What kind of meal is this?

F : It's korean style beef.

P : Well, I don't like beef. I'd like the chicken, please.

F : I'm sorry sir, but we are all out of chicken today. Now we only have beef left.

P : All right. I'll take the beef then.

F : Here you are. I apologize for not serving you what you like.

P : It's o.k.

F : Enjoy your meal, sir.

Dialogue 2

S : Stewardess P : Passenger

P : Excuse me. There is something in my meal.

S : Oh! I'm very sorry, sir. I'll get you a new meal right away.
wait a moment, please.

.....

S : Thank you for waiting. Here is another meal for you.
Would you care for some tea or coffee?

P : Tea, please.

S : Here you are. Would you like some lemon with your tea?

P : Yes, please.

Dialogue 3

S : Stewardess P : Passenger

S : Excuse me, ma'am. You look pale.

P : Yes, I don't feel very well.

S : I am sorry. What's wrong?

P : I feel like vomiting and a bit dizzy.
Do you have some medicine for me?
I am sensitive to air turbulence.

S : Do you need an airsickness bag?

P : Yes, please bring it to me with some medicine.

S : O.K. wait a minute, please.
Here you are. Take two tablets at one time.

P : I hope I feel better soon.

S : I hope so, too

Dialogue 4

S : Stewardess P : Passenger

P : Excuse me, how do I change channels?
S : Please push this button.

P : Excuse me, how do I turn on the reading light?
S : The button is right here.

P : How do I recline my seat?
S : Please push this button and lean back.

P : Excuse me, but I'm a little cold. Could you bring me a blanket?
S : Sure, Here is your blanket. Would you like hot water?

P : Yes, please give me some.
S : Would you like something to read?

P : Oh, that would be nice.
S : Here is a Newsweek. Have a pleasant flight, ma'am.

Air Service English Vocabulary

- Main Contract 주계약
- Main Dish 주요리
- Main Landing Gear 주착륙장치
- Main Runway 주활주로
- Main wing 주날개
- Maintainability 정비성
- Maintenance 정비정검
- Manual 교범
- Major Repair 주요 수리
- Maker 제작사
- Make a Reservation 예약하다
- Marker 이정표
- Material 재료
- Maximum Altitude 최대고도
- Maximum Capacity 최대수용인원
- Maximum Operation Speed 최대 운용속도
- Maximum Power 최대출력
- Mayday 긴급재난신호
- Meal 식사

- Mean Time 표준시
- Mechanic 정비사
- Military Aircraft 군용기
- Midnight flight 야간 항공기
- Monitor 감청
- Monsoon 계절풍
- Mountain Breeze 산풍
- Movement Area 이동지역

Interview Basic Questions

Answer the following questions briefly.

1. How different is it between our Airlines and another Airlines?

2. If you are failed this time, what will you do?

3. As a flight attendant, what is the most important characteristics?

4. What is good service?

Situation English Tips

What	kind of sort of type of	books music food clothes	do you	like? dislike?
Well, I	like dislike	science book(s). beef steak. classical music. korean food.		
Who(What)	is are	your the most	favorite	music(s)? book(s)? writer(s)?

That is a very difficult question, but perhaps Harry Porter.

Of course,	Harry Potter. korean food. romantic book.

I prefer	apples watching TV	to	oranges reading books

Translation

1	유머감각이 있는 편이라 분위기를 화기애애하게 띄우곤 합니다.	I have a good sense of humor. So create a very friendly atmosphere.
2	저는 아주 사교적이고 여행을 좋아합니다.	I'm very sociable and I love to travel.
3	저는 매우 외향적이고 사람을 좋아합니다.	I'm very outgoing and I like people.
4	저는 융통성 있고 느긋한 편입니다.	I'm flexible and easy going.
5	모든 일에 적극적이라고 봅니다.	I approach things very enthusiastically.
6	저는 항상 긍정적인 면을 바라보려고 노력합니다.	I am the type of person who always tries to see the positive side of things.
7	유머감각이 있고 함께하는게 재미있는 사람이라는 얘기를 많이 듣는 편입니다.	Everybody says I have a good sense of humor and I am fun to be with.

CHAPTER 7

Airline Interview English

I. How would you describe your personality?

1. I am a very enthusiastic, energetic young woman who's willing to try what the world has to offer. When I have traveled I've tried to experience as much of the local culture and meet as many local people as possible. My personality is such that I'm not scared of jumping in to unknown situations and trying new things. For example, when I was in Thailand I met some locals and stayed at their home in the countryside rather than going to the usual tourist traps.

2. I'm very open-minded to new ideas and I like meeting people. On top of that, I am also good at coping with stress. I can be seen at many social occasions and I blend into the environment rapidly. My friends tell me that they would like to see me get angry once because I never do.

3. I believe in learning and sharing new experiences and pushing myself to be a better person. I really love to discover new things and to broaden my horizons. When my friends traveled, they went on a package tour to Western Europe, whereas I traveled with the people I met on the trip and covered Eastern and Southern Europe where I was into less familiar territory.

4. I'm very sociable and get along great with other people. I love meeting new people for the first time and think I'm a great at mingling at social events. I like to bring my old friends into newer circles, too. Last year I made my shyest friend join a group of foreigners with me in Dongdaemun market. We met them on the bus there and translated for them and helped them get some bargains. Now we still hang out every few weeks. We have fun and it allows me to practice my English.

5. I'm a people person. I'm happiest when I can interact with others and help them. My previous experience in the service industry has convinced me that I'm at my best when I'm helping people and trying to make them happy and comfortable. I can't really see myself working in any other industry. When I worked as a waitress it was sometiomes physically demanding, but I got to meet lots of people, so it was much more rewarding than my office jobs.

6. I'm a problem solver. My friends are always coming to me for advice on all sorts of topics: personal and professional. They say I should be a counselor or therapist. Even my mother often asks me what I think when she has a big decision to make. I guess I'm a logical thinker and good seeing others' points of view. I can usually make people see that there is a simple solution to most problems.

7. My strong points are that I have a sense of humor and that I approach things positively and actively. I also mix with others very well. My weak point is that before I start doing something, I always worry too much about not doing it correctly. So I often lose my opportunities to excel.

8. I am an extremely confident, progressive and sociable person with a good sense of humor. I love meet people. Even when I was working as a guide in a museum I had a blast because I got to talk to people form all over the world and experience their cultures and their ways for a short time. And now I can say hello and goodbye in over twenty languages.

Ⅱ. Why do you want to become a flight attendant?

1. I think that working on a cabin crew will be interesting but not easy. Not only will I get to visit different places but I'll get to meet a lot of different people from different styles of life. Although a lot of the work seems demanding both physically and mentally, the variety of the work and the situations will keep me fresh and motivated.

2. I love meeting new people so I decided to work in the service industry. I've really enjoyed the work I've done so far in restaurants, hotels and convention centers. I've met a lot of new friends on the staffs and seen many interesting people among the customers. Unfortunately, it is difficult to earn a good living in these industries in Korea, and there isn't much opportunity for advancement for young women. So working on an airplane seems like the perfect job for me.

3. Obviously one of the benefits of becoming a flight attendant is the opportunity to travel. I've really enjoyed the few chances I've had to leave Korea and broaden my horizons, but as I need to work I don't get the chance that often. Traveling as part of my job will be a wonderful benefit, and I hope to experience as much of the world and as many different cultures as the job allows.

4. I want to become a flight attendant because I like the work that brings me in contact with people and that requires some physical activity. When I traveled on your airline I was impressed with the way the flight attendants worked. I decided that that's the kind of work I'd like to do.

Ⅲ. What do you think are important attributes for a flight attendant?

1. I think it is very important to be cheerful. A flight attendant can determine the mood of a travel experience for the passengers. If they are friendly and cheerful it is much more likely that the passengers will enjoy their journey.
   The most important things are awareness of passengers' needs and serving those needs with a friendly attitude. If I can anticipate the requirements of passengers with special needs I will be much better prepared to meet those needs when they arise. And it is important that those passengers feel comfortable and don't get embarrassed. I'm known for being friendly and discreet. So I believe I can meet passengers' needs without fuss or delay.

2. Being able to make the right decision and remaining calm while on duty, a flight attendant has many demands on their time and priority multi-task. This means that choosing the right course of action and time of action for given situations is very important. If the right decisions are made, problems and stress levels will remain low. However, when issues do come up, it is important to deal with them in the same calm, reasoned manner and to remain outwardly unflustered.
   I consider myself to be a logical thinker, good at deciding what is important.

3. Flexibility, good health, and physical strength seem to be very important. Some flights are very long, so physical weakness will lead to stress on body and mind. I think health is important in all areas of life, so I try to exercise regularly and eat well.

4. In order to serve many people it is necessary to be efficient and energetic. Working quickly and effectively will mean that there are fewer disruptions to passengers' movement and comfort on a flight. I think that I have the energy and focus to work like this.

IV. · How would you evaluate your ability to deal with conflict with passengers?
· If a passenger lost his temper on board, how would you deal with the situation?

1. I think that my temperament and manner are suited to avoiding and minimizing conflict with customers and coworkers. I think I'm a reasonable person, so I shouldn't cause too many problems. When a passenger is being unreasonable I have the ability to be apologetic and appeasing where necessary, and to be politely insistent in enforcement of policies when that is the right course of action. In my experience, when customers have had issues with me, I've always resolved them myself without involving my managers.

2. I have a lot of experience working in service industry jobs. So I've naturally had to deal with customer complaints. On the few occasions when I was at fault I apologized and tried to right the situation as quickly as possible. When the problem has been caused by someone else on staff, I've done the same on their behalf. When the conflict arises because the customer is very demanding or difficult, I try to calm them down by being reasonable and polite, but call in my superiors when the situation seems impossible to resolve or the customer is just being unreasonable.

V. Once you become a flight attendant, what kind of service would you like to offer?

1. I will try to make the atmosphere friendly and comfortable by smiling a lot and using kind words. If a passenger has a request, I will always try to fill it in a friendly and polite way, and not make them feel like they are being difficult.

2. Of course, I will provide the best possible service in a friendly and helpful way. Additionally, my language skills mean that I can talk to many passengers in their own language which will make them more comfortable. At the moment I can speak Korean, English and Mandarin well, and have basic Japanese and Arabic. I know how to greet, farewell and thank someone in other languages.

   I'll try to identify and satisfy the needs of every passenger in a polite, cheerful manner. I have experienced working in a home for disabled children, so I'll be able to take care of babies when needed, and can meet the needs of disabled passengers especially well. I even know basic sign language, Korean and American.

3. I've worked in a rest home and enjoy interacting with the elderly. I can make older passengers comfortable and talk to them and attend to their special needs.

4. I'll use the skills I learnt at school. I studied engineering and we learned how to look at a problem or challenge and make the right decisions through logic and reason and by following the right procedures. I think that this discipline will help me deal with the challengers of being a flight attendant.

Vocabulary

- Observation Car 전망차
- Obstruction Light 장애물 표시등
- Off Day 비번일
- Off–season Fare 비수기 요금
- Oil cooler 오일냉각기
- On Board 탑승
- One–Stop 일괄처리
- One Way Fare 편도요금
- Orientation 사전교육
- Out bound 외항
- Outlet 출구
- Over Load 과적
- Overview 개관

Interview Basic Questions

❀ **Answer the following questions briefly.**

1. Have you been a leader?
   what brought you to that position?

2. How do you make people accept your idea?

3. What do you think about your appearance?

4. How do you think about your health?

5. What gives you stress?

Situation English Tips

Would you mind	if I go home early today?
	giving me a ride home tonight? if I use the bathroom?
Could you	give me something to drink?

Yes,	of course. certainly. go ahead.

No,	not at all. of course not.

Excuse me

May Can Could	I ask you a question?
	I get by, please?
Let me through, please. Clear the way, please.	

Translation

1	저는 더 많은 책임을 맡길 원합니다.	I'm looking for more responsibilities.
2	제 경력을 더욱 발전시키고 싶습니다.	I want to advance my career further.
3	제 분야에서 인정을 받을 것이라 확신합니다.	I'm sure I would be recognized in my field.
4	저는 항상 모범이 되려고 합니다.	I always make every effort to lead by example.
5	모범을 보이는 것이 아주 중요하다고 생각합니다.	I think setting an example is very important.
6	승객들이 소중함을 느끼도록 한 분 한 분을 귀하게 여기는 고객중심의 서비스를 제공하겠습니다.	I would like to provide every single passenger with my customer oriented service, so that the passengers would feel they are valuable and I am there to serve them as well.

CHAPTER 8

About self Introduction

영문이력서 Resume

영문이력서는 영어로 Resume 또는 Curriculum vitae라고 하며 외항사인 경우에 영문이력서를 요구하게 되는데 각 항공사가 원하는 인재상에 적합한 학력, 경력, 자격, 성격 등을 중점적으로 기재한다.

영문이력서 작성방법

• Personal Data

Name(이름)

Address(주소)

: 영문주소는 한글주소와 반대로 작성하는데 번지, 동, 구(면), 시(도), 우편번호 순으로 적는다.

• Phone Number(전화번호)

: 자택번호나 모바일 연락처를 국가번호와 함께 적는다. (예: +82 10 5432 1122)

E-mail (이메일주소)

• Job Objective

지원하는 직종과 업무를 기재하고 직업목표 적는다.

• Education

최근 졸업 순으로 시작해서 과거 순으로 최종 학력을 적고 전공, 부전공, 취득학위 명을 기재한다.

• Experiences

최근 경력부터 작성하며 회사명, 소재지, 직급, 근무 기간, 업무내용 등을 구체적으로 기재한다.

• Skills

공인된 자격증이나 면허증, 특기사항을 적는다.

• Activities

동아리활동, 자원봉사활동 등 학교에서의 대내외적 특별활동 사항을 적으면 된다.

• Honors and Awards

교내외적 행사의 수상경력이나 표창경력 또는 상벌 사항을 기록한다.

• References

'Available on request'로 간략히 기재하고 별도 요청이 있을 때 제출한다. 추천인은 자신의 능력과 자질을 보증할 수 있는 제3자로 경력자는 직장상사나 책임자가 적당하며 학생이라면 지도교수의 이름, 주소, 직위, 연락처를 기재한다.

샘플 이력서

Uni Kim

45 Jangan-dong, Pyeongtaek, Korea

Home: 031-610-1234 Cell: 010-8880-1234 Email: unikim@hanmail.net

• Objective

Obtain the position of flight attendant with Korean Air customer service skills.

• Summary of Qualifications

* Major of Airline service department in university

* TOEIC 780 : able to interpret and translate.

* Proficient with computer reservation system of airline ticket.

* A grade holder of Judo.

* Certificate of Sign Language.

* Over three years of experience in the customer service industry.

* Studied English in the U.S. for 9 months.

* Good at English conversation.

- Work Experience

Cafeteria of university at Korea : Korea, March 2010 ~ August 2010

* Part time job as a cashier and assistant
* Improved English skill and learned cultures of other country.
* Palza Hotel : Seoul, January 2010, August 2010

Part time job as a waitress

* Gang nam Wedding Hall : Seoul, January 2009
  - Worked on weekends
  - Assitant of Wedding
  - Customer Service

- Education

* Will be graduated from Kookje university.
* Majored Tourism & Airline Service Department.
* Graduated from Songtan high school in February, 2007

- Awards and Activities

Grand prize in Kookje English speech contest spring semester of 2010.

Department Scholarship

worked as a volunteer at Songtan International Center. - July 2010.

- References

Available on request.

커버레터 (Cover Letter) 작성법

• Cover Letter Ⅰ

Example :

Dear Sir / Madam.

I would like to express my strong interest in the position of Cabin Crew member.

My major is Airline Service, and I became strongly motivated after I completed the Cabin Crew Experience program with Asiana Airlines. I feel that I am a very suitable person for this profession. To be a professional service person, I completed an internship at the Shilla Hotel as a trainee. Furthermore, I volunteered as a Multi-Cultural Festival interpreter to improve my inter-personal communication skills with people from other cultures.

I am a very flexible person who can help organize and lead a team based on my experiences in taking charge of my department. I am a resourceful person, so I can bring out the best in other people, irrespective of their nationality. Also, I am a calm person. So I would deal with any emergency or crisis by keeping my presence of mind. I believe that I can be an asset to assist harmony and growth by working in your company, Global Airlines.

A copy of my resume and photographs are enclosed for your consideration.

Should you require further information, please feel free to contact me.

I look forward to hearing from you in the near future to schedule an interview at your convenience. I appreciate your consideration.

Sincerely yours

Uni Kim

Enclosure : Resume

• Cover Letter Ⅱ

Dear Sir or Madam:

Your advertisement for a flight attendant, appearing on your company website, caught my attention because of my interest in a flight attendant career with Korean Air. I am currently employed with the Airline Service department at (kookje) University.

I have had a dream to become a flight attendant since I was 15 years old. I really like to meet people and I feel happy when I see some people who are impressed with my help. Also, I have the ability to cooperate across various countries, and cultures, along with a high level of flexibility and willingness. I think Korean Air is looking for someone who can give customers the best service, with the goals of customer satisfaction and impression, and this is consistent with my personality. I believe being a flight attendant is my divinely appointed work in life.

I am impressed with the outstanding reputation of Korean Air and know I possess the enthusiasm and initiative that would allow me to be an excellent representative of Korean Air.

I look forward to hearing form you, and I have enclosed a resume with the details of my qualifications for your review. Please contact me(010-8880-1234) to arrange an interview at your earliest convenience so that we can discuss how my qualifications can contribute to Korean Air.

Sincerely,

Uni Kim

Self-Introduction

Thank you for giving me the opportunity to introduce myself. I'm Ji–soo Leem and I am majoring in the Department of Airline Service at Kookje University. Through my major, I've learned communication skills, a variety of activities, and gained much knowledge related to my major.

I have completed a First–Aid Instructor and Airline Reservation/Ticketing course in preparation to be a cabin crew member. Through these courses, I have learned how to deal with emergency situations which is one of the qualifications as a part of the cabin crew.

As a freshman in university, I participated in an internship program at the Travellers' Hotel. At that time, I was in charge of serving in the Food and Beverage division. Therefore, I've learned how to handle customer's complaints, interact with people, and to show my service skills.
Also, I participated in an English speaking club and I was honored with a grand prize in the English speech contest.
One of the most important requirements is to be healthy, so I often go hiking up a mountain behind my dormitory. When I was in high school, I was the winner of a marathon race. This is a result of my regular exercise, which has also given me confidence and good physical health.

Therefore, I truly believe I would be a great asset to this company and help it to stay competitive.

• 성격을 표현하는 단어들

Compassionate	Creative	Kind	Affectionate	Extroverted
Easy-going	Generous	Reliable	Punctual	Responsible
Smart	Sympathetic	Committed	Supportive	Efficient
Friendly	Active	Caring	Ambitious	Outgoing
Open-minded	Optimistic	Sincere	Sensitive	Polite
Courteous	Patient	Sociable	Confident	Adaptable
Passionate	Mature	Enthusiastic	Flexible	High-spirited
Experienced	Intellectual	Dedicated	Cooperative	Hardworking

Write about your Self-Introduction.

English Vocabulary

- National air space 영공
- Nationality 국적
- Navigation 항법
- Navigator 항법사
- Necessary speed 필요속도
- Negative pressure 부압
- News stand 신문대
- Night Auditor 야간감사
- Night cap 위생모자
- Night Flight 야간비행
- No show(er) 미탑승(객)
- No Tax card 면세카드
- Normal Flight 정상비행
- Not for Drinking '먹는물아님'
- Note 어음

Interview Basic Questions

※ **Answer the following questions briefly.**

1. How do you keep your body health and strong?

2. Tell me about your daily life.

3. What makes you happy?

4. What makes you sad?

5. When was the saddest(or happiest) moment in your life?

Situation English Tips

Would you like Do you want	a drink? something to eat?
How about Do you feel like	drinking a cup of coffee?
Why don't you	drink something? buy some ties?

<table>
<tr><td>Yes,</td><td>please.
I'd love to.</td><td colspan="2">Thank you.</td></tr>
<tr><td colspan="4">That sounds good.</td></tr>
<tr><td>No,</td><td>thank you.</td><td rowspan="2">but</td><td rowspan="2">I can't</td></tr>
<tr><td colspan="2">I'd really like to</td></tr>
</table>

Translation

NO	Korean sentence	English sentence
	Competence	
1	저는 대화가 모든 갈등을 완화하는데 핵심적인 요소라고 생각합니다.	I think communication is the key competence to ease up most conflicts.
2	무슨 일이 잘못되었는지 알기 전까지는 화내는 것을 자제합니다.	I try not to get upset until I find out what went wrong.
3	모든 에너지를 해결책을 찾는 데로 쏟아 붓습니다.	I channel all my energy toward a solution.
4	저는 우선 문제의 원인을 알아내려고 합니다.	The first thing I try to fine out is the cause of a problem.
5	즐거운 분위기를 만드는 것이 가장 중요하다고 생각합니다.	I think the most important thing is to create an upbeat environment.
6	제가 하는 일에 자부심을 느끼고 싶습니다.	l like to be proud of what I do.
7	될 수 있는 한 최고가 되고 싶습니다.	l like to be the best that I can be.

PART 2

Tourism Service English

CHAPTER 9

Tourist Information

Dialogue 1

C : Information Clerk T : Tourist

C : May I help you?

T : Yes, please. I'd like to go somewhere around here. Especially (Nam-San Tower)

C : Have you ever been here before?

T : No, I'm a stranger here myself. How do I get there?

C : You can take a taxi or a bus.

T : How much is the fare?

C : The taxi fare is about 8,000 won and 3,000won for the bus.

T : Oh, I see. I'd like to take a bus.

C : There is a shuttle bus every thirty minutes.

T : Could you tell me where I get the bus?

C : In front of this building.

T : Thank you for your help.

C : Have a nice trip.

Dialogue 2

C : clubhouse clerk	G : Guest

C : Lake Hills Golf course. May I help you?

G : I'd like to make a reservation for Sunday. When is the earliest opening time?

C : Well, let me check.

....

Thank you for waiting.

The earliest opening is 10 O'clock in the morning. sir.

G : How about 9 O'clock ?

C : I'm sorry, sir. We are fully booked until 9:45.

G : Oh, I see. Then I'll take the 10 O'clock tee time.

C : May I have your name and phone number?

G : David Kim and my phone number is 010-8880-1234.

C : How many people in your party?

G : Four people.

C : All right, sir. Your tee off time is at 10 on this coming Sunday morning.

G : Thanks a lot.

Dialogue 3

C : Clerk　　　　T : Tourist

T : I want to rent a car. Why type of car do you have?

C : We have small, mid-size, full size, and vans.

T : How much do you charge for a van?

C : Our weekend special rate is $40 a day with the insurance coverage. It's 10% off.

T : That's fine. I'll take it.

C : Can I have your ID card?

T : Here it is.

C : How will you be paying?

T : By credit card.

C : Sign here, please. The car will be ready for you in the parking lot after 30 minutes. And also make sure you fill it up.

T : O.k. I see.

Dialogue 4

T : Tourist	D : Driver

D : Where are you going today, sir?

T : Could you get me to the London Hotel?

D : No problem. Where are you from?

T : I'm korean. I've just arrived here.

D : Is this your first visit to England?

T : No, I was here last month because of my business. How is the traffic at the moment?

D : The traffic is not so good in rush hour.

T : I am in a hurry. I have a very important meeting in the morning.
We should drive quickly.

D : O.k. I will try.

Vocabulary

- Package Tour 포괄여행
- Paging service 호출서비스
- Pain killer 진통제
- Pamplet 소책자
- Panorama 전경, 광경
- Paper cup 종이컵
- Parachute 낙하산
- Passenger List 승객명단
- Peel 껍질 벗기다
- Perfume 향수
- Permanent Address 본적
- Personal Belongings 개인소지품
- Pick up 차를 태우다
- Pillow 베개
- Pitcher 물주전자
- Premium 고급의
- Proposal 제안서

Interview Basic Questions

Answer the following questions briefly.

1. Have you ever been disappointed with someone?

2. Tell me about your best friend.

3. How do you make friends?

4. What was the greatest mistake in your life?

5. What did you learn from those mistakes?

Situation English Tips

Don't (Never)	touch me! move! say like that. be late again. forget to come early tomorrow.

Mind	you! (명심해, 잘들어) the step! (발밑 조심해) out! (정신차려)

What do you think of What's your opinion of How do you feel about	smoking in a car? shouting in the street?

I think that In my opinion As I see it My view is that	it is not good. there is some problem.

Translation

1	저는 아르바이트를 하면서 사람대하는 능력을 길렀습니다.	I acquired inter-personal skills through my part time job.
2	고객서비스 분야에서 일하는데 깊은 관심이 있습니다.	I am deeply interested in working in the customer service area.
3	사람들은 배려하고 남의 말을 잘 들어주는 편이라 고객들과 좋은 관계를 쌓을 수 있었습니다.	My concern for people and good listening skills helped me build strong relationships with customers.
4	저는 긍정적이고 지속적인 고객관계를 형성하는데 기여하겠습니다.	I will contribute to creating positive and lasting customer relationships.
5	저는 일을 통해 실제 사회경험을 키우는데 집중했습니다.	I have focused my energy on work and obtaining real-world experience.
6	저는 항상 고객의 입장에서 생각해보려고 합니다.	I always try to put myself in the customer's shoes.

Restaurant and Shopping

CHAPTER 10

Dialogue 1

W : Waiter G : Guest

W : Good evening, sir.

How many people are in your party?

G : Four all together.

W : Where would you like to sit?

By the window or further back?

G : Window seats, please. I'd like to see the good view.

W : O.k. I see. This way, please.

....

Here is the menu.

May I take your order?

G : What is your recommendation for today?

W : How about the steak?

G : Good, I'll take it.

W : How would you like the meat done?

G : Medium-well done, please.

W : What would you like to drink?

We have beer and wine.

G : Red wine, please.

Dialogue 2

W : Waitress G : Guest

W : Is there anything wrong, ma'am?

G : Yes, I ordered my steak medium well-done, but mine is too rare.

W : Oh, I'm sorry. I'll take it back to the kitchen and get you another one.

G : That is not all. I found a fly in my dish. And my vegetables are too salty.

W : I'm awfully sorry. I'll speak to the chef and bring you some mild vegetables.

....

Here are new ones. These are special services for you. We are very sorry for the inconvenience. Please accept our apologizes.

We will make sure this doesn't happen again.

Dialogue 3

C : Clerk T : Tourist

C : Good afternoon, ma'am?
Is there anything particular you're looking for?

T : I'm looking for a jacket.

C : How about this blue one?

T : Do you have a white one?

C : Yes, we do. Please try it on.

T : Oh, this one is too small for me.
Do you have a larger one?

C : Sure, here you go.

T : Do you think this looks good on me?

C : I think it looks good, but how about you?

T : I like it. How much is it?

C : It's 100$.

T : O.k. I'll take it. Would you gift-wrap it for me?

C : Certainly. ma'am.

Dialogue 4

C : Clerk	T : Tourist

C : What can I help you with, ma'am?

T : I'm just looking.

C : All right, ma'am. If you need any help, please let me know.

T : O.k.

....

Oh! This shirt looks good. What colors do you have?

C : We have red, yellow, blue and white.

T : Can I try on the red one?

C : Sure. Here you go.

T : It is too large for me. And the red color doesn't look good on me.
Please show me another one.

C : Here is the white one.

T : Oh, I like it. How much is it?

C : It's 80$.

T : Oh, it is a little expensive. Could you come down a little?

C : Sorry, we sell at fixed prices.

T : I see, I'll take it. Please gift-wrap it for me.

C : Certainly, ma'am.

Vocabulary

- Radiator 라디에이터, 방열기
- Raft 구명보트
- Real Time 실시간
- Receipt 영수증
- Reconfirm 재확인하다(예약)
- Refund 환불
- Reinforcement 강화, 보강
- Reissue 재발급
- Requirement 요구조건
- Rescue 구조
- Reservation 예약
- Resolution 해결
- Resort 휴양지
- Response 응답
- Round Trip 왕복여행

Interview Basic Questions

※ **Answer the following questions briefly.**

1. Have you ever worked in the service field?

2. If you have, how long did you work there and what were your duties?

3. What did you do to satisfy customers?

4. Tell me about one of your most memorable customers.

5. What's your philosophy of life?

Situation English Tips

You look	tired. upset. worried.	What's	the matter? wrong? up? the problem?
Why don't you	go to see a doctor? go home and take a rest? tell me your problem?		
I am sorry	I am late. I made a mistake. for the inconvenience. I was wrong. it's all my fault.		
Oh,	that's all right. don't worry about that. it doesn't matter. never mind. forget it!		

Translation

1	어떠한 상황에도 적응할 수 있고 뜻밖의 일도 예측할 수 있는 능력이 중요하다는 것을 배웠습니다.	I quickly learned the importance of being able to adapt to any situation and expecting the unexpected.
2	고객의 불만을 개인적으로 받아들여서는 안 된다고 생각합니다.	I shouldn't take things like customers' complaints personally.
3	팀원들로부터 함께 일하기 좋은 최고의 팀원이라는 얘기를 항상 들었습니다.	My team members always told me I was the best person they worked with.
4	저는 팀의 일원으로 일하는 것을 좋아합니다.	I like to work as part of a team.
5	저는 최우수 사원상을 받았습니다.	I was named Employee of the Year.
6	저는 항상 프로젝트에서 가장 어려운 과업을 먼저 처리하려고 노력합니다.	I always try to tackle the most difficult tasks of a project first.
7	고객서비스분야의 교육과 경험이 있습니다.	I've had a lot of customer service training and experience.

Tour Guide English

CHAPTER 11

Dialogue 1

G : Guide T : Tourist

G : Good morning, Mr. Robert. Are you ready to go sightseeing today?

T : Sure. Where are we going?

G : We are going to look around Seoul on a city tour bus. It stops at 28 major places around Seoul. And it provides language service in English, Japanese and Chinese.

T : It sounds good.

G : Here is the course schedule for the tour bus. Here is Gyeongbok palace. This palace was built in 1395 by king Taejo, founder of the Joseon Dynasty. The royal family lived here.

T : Oh, I see. And where are we heading now?

G : We're going to walk to Insa-dong.

T : How long will it take from here?

G : It will take about 10 minutes on foot. If you're interested in antiques, you will enjoy it.

Dialogue 2

T : Tourist   C : Clerk   G : Guide

G : Our next stop is Namdaemun Market opened in 1964. It is the largest traditional market in Korea with various goods in stores. While Dongdaemun Market is a mecca for fashion, Namdaemun market offers a variety of clothes, glasses, kitchenware, toys, fishing equipment, stationery, accessories, hats and so on.

T : If so, I'd like to buy shoes.
C : How may I help you?

T : Do you have size 10 in blue?
C : Wait a minute. Here you are. Try this on.

T : I think it fits me well. How much is it?
C : it is on sale for 60$.

T : Could you come down a little?
C : I'm sorry, but it's a sale price. How would you like to pay?
T : In cash, please.

Dialogue 3

T : Tourist G : Guide

G : Today we are going to a Folk village in Yongin.

T : How long does it take from Seoul to the Folk village?

G : It takes about an hour by car. And it is a living museum that recreates the lifestyle of several centuries ago. It offers various performances for example folk music, dance, tight–rope acrobatics, traditional weddings, seesaw jumping and many other special events. Oh, here we are.

T : Are these houses built in a korean traditional style?

G : Yes, they are typical of the late Joseon Dynasty.
This is a house where yangban, the gentry used to live.

T : I'd like to see some traditional events.

G : Let me ask at information if there's any events today.
....
Oh, they say that there is tight–rope acrobatics. Let's go see.

Dialogue 4

G : Guide T : Tourist

G : Welcome to Jeju Island!
Is this your first visit?

T : No, actually it's my second time. But I didn't have much time to see many places. It was my business trip. So at this time I'd like to look arround many famous places here.

G : Good! Are you ready to explore the rest of Jeju Island now?

T : Of course!

G : We're going to go to Jeju Folk village now. It is located at the foot of Mt. Halla. There are old houses, fortress sites, tombstones and so on. And the life style of Jeju Islanders 100years ago is kept alive.

T : Oh, I see. And I'd like to see Mt. Halla.

G : It's 1950 meters high and a sleeping volcano.

T : Sounds interesting. Let's climb it!

G : You can see a spectacular view of sunrise and sunset there!

Vocabulary

- Safety 안전
- Sanitary-napkin 생리용품
- Scale 저울
- Seat back 좌석원위치
- Second pilot 부조종사
- Security Check-in 보안수속
- Separation 분리
- Serious Injury 중상
- Shuttle 왕복선, 정기운행 교통수단
- Side by Side 나란히, 병렬로
- Sightseeing 관광
- Sky shop 기내 면세점
- Smog 연기와 안개의 혼합물
- Snack Bar 간이식당
- Soft Drink 청량음료
- Souvenir shop 기념품점
- Steward 남자승무원

Interview Basic Questions

※ **Answer the following questions briefly.**

1. Have you ever been to another country?
   If yes, why did you go there?

2. If you have a chance to go abroad, which country would you like to go the most? why?

3. Tell me your most memorable trip.

4. What was the most difficult thing in your travel?

5. Have you worked in a team before?

Situation English Tips

What are you	going to do? planning to do? intending to do?
what are you thinking of doing?	
I'm going to be I hope to be I intend to be	a flight attendant. a teacher
I was going to, I had planned to, I had hoped to,	but I've changed my mind. I've failed.

Translation

1	대학교때, 리츠칼튼호텔에서 인턴십프로그램에 참여했습니다.	During my college days, I participated in an internship program at the Ritz Carlton Hotel.
2	싱가폴로 여행을 다녀왔습니다.	I went to Singapore to sight-seeing.
3	호텔 인턴십 프로그램은 아주 유익한 경험이었고 저에게 훌륭한 배움의 기회를 주었습니다.	The hotel internship program was a most rewarding experience, and it gave me an excellent learning opportunity.
4	그러한 경험으로 저는 강한 리더십과 커뮤니케이션 기술 및 팀워크에 대해 배울 수 있었습니다.	From those activities, I learned strong leadership skills, communication skills and teamwork.
5	해외에서의 공부는 제게 다른 나라들에 대한 새로운 지식을 주었으며 세상에 대한 견해를 넓히는 계기가 되었습니다.	Studying abroad gave me new knowledge of other countries, and enlarged my view of the world.
6	저는 여행을 통해서 세상과 인생을 바라보는 관점을 더욱 넓힐 수 있었습니다.	I was able to broaden my view of the world and life through traveling.
7	아르바이트로 얻은 경험은 정말 값을 매길 수 없이 소중한 것이었습니다.	The experience I gained from my part-time job is priceless.

8	봉사활동은 제게 세상을 보는 관점을 넓혀주었고 세상을 좀 더 인간적으로 포용 할 수 있도록 도와주었습니다.	My volunteer activities broadened my view of the world and helped me embrace a humanistic view of the world.
9	그 인턴십 프로그램으로 저는 좀 더 효과적으로 문제에 접근하고 해결하는 방법을 배울 수 있었습니다.	From the internship program I learned how to approach and solve problems effectively.

Situation English

CHAPTER 12

Traffic

Dialogue 1

P : Passenger D : Driver

P : Excuse me. Is this bus for Kookje college?

D : No, you take the bus 55 and get off the bus after 5 stops. And then you can get in front of the main building of the college.

P : How often does the bus run?

D : It is running every twenty minutes.

P : Oh, that's too long in between Is there any other way to get there?

D : You can take a taxi over there. It takes only 10 minutes by taxi.

P : Oh, I see. Thank you for your kindness.

D : You're welcome.

* 교통이 혼잡하다: The traffic is bumper to bumper.
every twenty minutes(20분 마다)

Directions

Dialogue 2

A : Tourist 1　　B : Tourist 2　　C : Clerk

A : Excuse me, where can I get to the nearest pay phone?

B : I'm sorry, but I am a stranger here, too. Why don't you ask the information desk?

A : Where is the information desk?

B : It's down the hall and on the right.

A : Thank you.

C : May I help you?

A : Yes, please. How do I get to the nearest pay phone?

C : There is one a couple of blocks from here.

A : And also, How far is the post office?

C : It's not that far.

A : Do I have to take the bus?

C : No, you don't have to.
Turn left onto Jongno and then go straight until you hit Sejong street. You will see the post office on your left.

A : Thank you very much.

Bank

Dialogue 3

O : officer   G : Guest

O : Welcome, Sir. How may I help you?

G : I'd like to open an account.

O : Which one do you need, a checking account or a savings account?

G : I'll need it to pay my monthly bills.

O : It sounds like you need a checking account. It is interest bearing but the interest rate is relatively low.

G : OK, that will be fine. And also I want to wire $ 1000.

O : Can I see your ID card?

G : Sure. here it is.

Medical

Dialogue 4

D : Doctor	P : Patient

D : Good morning. How can I help you?

P : I have an upset stomach.

D : Let me take a look.
Do you have fever and diarrhea?

P : Yes. I have some chills.

D : Oh, that's too bad.
You may get diarrhea from the wrong foods.

P : I had some raw fish and ice drinks yesterday.

D : I'll give you a prescription. Please take a rest all day if possible.
And come again after two days, if you don't feel better.

P : Thanks a lot.

Vocabulary

- Take-off 이륙
- Tax Free 면세
- Temporary visitor 일시방문자
- Terminology 전문용어
- Thermostat 온도조절기
- Time Table 운행시간표
- Tourist Information 관광안내소
- Trainee 실습생
- Travel Agency 여행사
- Traveler's check 여행자수표
- Vacation 휴가
- Valid 유효한
- Vaccination 예방접종
- Validity 유효기간
- Valuables 귀중품
- Ventilation 환풍
- Visa Application 비자신청
- Waiting List 대기자 명단
- Wind shield 바람막이
- Yellow Card 예방접종 증명서

Interview Basic Questions

❀ **Answer the following questions briefly.**

1. Have you ever used our airline?
   How was the service?

2. What do you think of service mind?

3. What is your salary expectation?

4. How would you handle an irate passenger?

5. Why did you apply for our company?

Situation English Tips

What will you do if you get the job?
what if you won the flight attendant job?

Well, if that happened	I would go out and celebrate.
I think I suppose	I'll be happy.

Why didn't you Why couldn't you have	let me know? call me? phoned to let me know?

I'm sorry, there was an accident. I wasn't able to, something happened.
please understand me.

Translation

1	승무원은 승객들이 여행을 즐길 수 있도록 비행내내 편안함과 휴식을 제공해야 합니다.	Flight attendants should know how to keep people comfortable and relaxed throughout the flight so that they can enjoy the trip.
2	제 직업에서 가장 중요한 것 중에 하나가 승객들이 미래에 다시 우리 항공사를 이용하고 싶도록 만드는 것입니다.	I think one of the most important things in my job is to make passengers want to fly with up again in the future.
3	모든 승객들이 비행 중에 편안하고 즐거운 시간이 되도록 하는 것이 가장 중요하다고 생각합니다.	I believe the most important thing is to make sure that all the passengers have a comfortable and enjoyable time during their flight.
4	저는 국제선에서 일하고 싶고 힘든 일도 감당할 준비가 되어 있습니다.	I want to work on international flights and I'm willing to make on a tough schedule.
5	저는 귀사가 세계 최고의 항공사 중 하나라는 것을 잘 알고 있습니다.	I know your company has a reputation for being one of the best airlines in the world.
6	저는 기내음식 또한 아주 훌륭하다고 알고 있습니다.	I also know your in-flight meals are really delicious.
7	5년 후에 저는 팀의 리더를 맡을 거라고 생각합니다.	In five years, I see myself being a team leader.

8	저는 승객들이 안전하고 편안한 비행을 할 수 있도록 좋은 여행 파트너가 되고 싶습니다.	I'd like to become like a great traveling partner to provide passengers with a comfortable and safe flight.
9	좋은 팀워크는 승객들에게 좋은 서비스로 이어진다고 믿습니다.	I believe good teamwork leads to good service for passengers.
10	승객들의 만족을 끌어낼 수 있도록 승무원은 자신이 대접받고 싶은 만큼 승객들을 대해야 합니다.	In order to satisfy passengers with service cabin crews should treat passengers like they want to be treated.

Tourism & Airline Service English Tourism & Airline Service English Tourism & Airline Service English Tourism & Airline Service English

PART 3

부 록

외국항공사 영어인터뷰 기출문제

1. Can I have your name please?

2. Would you please introduce yourself?

3. How tall are you? What is your height?

4. How heavy are you? What is your weight?

5. What is your father's job?

6. What does your father do for a living? Are you proud of his job?

7. Describe your father's personality.

8. What does you mother's character like?

9. Do you help your mother a lot?

10. Are you a student? / Do you go to school? Which school do you go to? If not, which university or college did you graduate form?

11. What is[was] your major? / What did you specialize in? What do you think of your major? / Why did you choose it as your major?

12. Did you join in any group of extracurricular activities during your school days?
What position did you hold [take up] in the group? What did you learn through the activities? / Did you take part in any voluntary activities for the community?

13. How long does it take to get here from Pusan? How did you come here? / What did you do[think] in[on] the train[bus; airplane]?

14. Do you spend much time talking to your family? If so, what is the topic about? If not, why?

15. What is the philosophy[motto] of your family? / Who set up that motto? / Do you try to live by that motto?

16. How is your health? / Have you ever been hospitalized? Have you been seriously sick? If so, why? For how long?

17. Do you have any visible scars on your body?

18. What do you do to keep yourself fit[in good shape]?

19. The job of a stewardess requires good health and much patience. Are you used to standing for a long time?

20. What is your hobby?

21. What is your talent? What are you good at? / Can you do something that many others can't do? Do you have any licenses or qualification certificates?

22. What do you think your personality is like? What do other people say about your character? Would you describe yourself as reserved or outgoing?

23. Tell me your strong points and weak points.

24. Out of 100 points, how many points would you give to yourself any why?

25. Can you introduce yourself? Please tell me about yourself.

26. Have you ever traveled[been] abroad[overseas]? If so, where to, for how long and what for?

27. Which country would you like to visit[travel]? Why there?

28. I need to lose my weight. What would you suggest me to do?

29. How do you usually spend your free time? What do you do when you are free? What do you usually do in weekends? What did you do last weekend? What is your plan after this interview? What do you plan to do this weekend?

30. Do you enjoy cooking? / What can you cook well? How do you make it? / Can you give me the recipe?

31. Do you know how Chollado food different from that of Kyoungsangdo?

32. How often do you help you mother with her housework? What do you do to help her? / How do you help her?

33. Please name a person, besides your parents, that respect most. / Why do you respect him[her]?

34. What kind of books do you enjoy reading? What is the most impressive book you have read so far? Why was it so impressive to you? Was it a bestseller?

35. What kind of movies do you like? What was the most impressive movie you've seen so far? / Who is your favorite movie[TV] star?

36. What kind of music do you like? Who is your favorite singer?

37. What is your blood type?

38. What is a friend to you? / How do you define a friend? What is your definition of a friend?

39. Tell me about your best friend and how you help each other.

40. Do you have a boyfriend? If so, tell me something about your boyfriend.

41. A handsome[good–looking] passenger asks you to dinner. Would you accept his invitation?

42. How do you think about marrying someone who is not a Korean?

43. What type of a man would you marry?

44. What is[was] your favorite subject at school? What subject did[do] you hate to study? Why?

45. Who paid for your education?

46. Did you have any part–time job? Where at? For how long? / What was the most difficult thing working the part–time job? / What did the job make you realize?

47. Did you have a full–time job? If you did, why did you quit the job?

48. If you are hired, how do you think your majoring subject can contribute to your work as a stewardess?

49. You are a student and if you are hired, what will you do with your schooling now?

50. If you suddenly have 500,000 won, what will you do with it. [how] will you spend it?

51. After you are hired and get your first pay, what would you purchase first with it and why?

52. If you fail to be hired this time, will you try for the second time?

53. How many times do you look at yourself in the mirror everyday and what do you check?

54. What basic principle do you apply to your life?

55. What do you expect from your future?

56. Do you believe that you are qualified to become a flight attendant?

57. Why do you want to be a stewardess? / Why did you decide to become a flight attendant?

58. What is your impression on a stewardess?

59. What do you think are some important characteristics for a flight attendant?

60. What do you think are the good parts and the bad parts in working as a stewardess?

61. Would you agree that it is the responsibility for the flight attendant to keep the aircraft clean?

62. How would you conduct yourself in case of emergency during flight?

63. Have you ever flown with Singapore Airlines? If yes, tell me how you enjoyed the flight. Is there anything you would like to suggest for our better service?

64. Why did you apply for our airlines? What made you apply for a job in our company?

65. Tell me where and how you learned about the job opening here?

66. Have you applied for a job in our company? What have you done to prepare for this test? / How have you prepared for this interview?

67. What would you say to the passenger who is smoking while the 'NO SMOKING' sign is on?

68. You spilled tomato juice or hot coffee on a passenger due to sudden turbulence. What would you say to the passenger?

69. What would you do if a heavily drunken passenger asks for more alcoholic drinks?

70. What would you do if an economy-class passenger asks for first-class meal?

71. What would you do if a passenger gets angry with you with no clear reason or a passenger speaks a strange language to you?

72. What if a passenger pinches or touches your hips[buttocks]?

73. How would you react if our company new policy is to massage the passengers in the cabin or sing to amuse them?

74. What do your family and friends say about your intention [plan] to become a stewardess?

75. If you are hired by us, you will have to live[stay] abroad where many things are different and strange. Do you think you can adapt yourself to new circumstances easily?

76. How long do you intend[plan] to work with us? / Would you continue working even after you are married? / What if your husband has different opinion and opposes to your intention?

77. Tell me what you are wearing today.

78. What is the weather like today? What is the weather forecast for tomorrow?

79. Which season are we in now? / In which months is it cold[hot] in Korea? / In which season is Christmas in Korea?

80. What holiday is (on) October 3rd in Korea?

81. Where did you learn English? Do you speak any other foreign languages besides English? If so, can you introduce yourself or sing a song in that language?

82. Have you studied [Did you study] at any special institute to become a stewardess? / What did you learn there? / Was it helpful for you to prepare to become a stewardess?

83. Assuming [Supposing] that you are a stewardess and your senior staff is much younger than you are, what would your attitude(towards him[her]) be?

84. How many TV channels are available in Pusan and what are they?

85. What does EBS[LATA, ICAO] stand for?

86. Tell us what you've done since you got up this morning.

87. What is your favorite holiday? Why?

88. What is your favorite food? Why?

89. How did you celebrate your last birthday?

90. What is happiness to you? When was the happiest [saddest] moment so far in your life?

91. What do you do when you are angry?

92. Tell us about the most valuable possession. Why is it so valuable to you?

93. Tell us the major current events published in today's newspaper.

94. How much is the city local bus fare in Pusan[Daegu]?

95. Which places would you recommend a foreigner who wants to go sightseeing in Korea? Why there?

96. What is the population of Pusan and Korea?

97. What are the major tourist attractions of Pusan[Daegu]?

98. Where is Jeju Island located?

99. What is the currency and the exchange rate for US dollar in Korea?

100. Do you want to know anything more about our company?

저자약력

정 은 주

- 영문학박사(세종대학교 대학원 영어영문학과, 영미문학전공)
  현) 국제대학교 관광경영계열 부교수

고 인 숙

- 영문학박사(성균관대학교 대학원 영어영문학과, 영미문학전공)
  현) 국제대학교 관광경영계열 부교수

Tourism & Airline Service English

2012년 8월 20일 초판1쇄 인쇄
2012년 8월 25일 초판1쇄 발행

저 자 정은주 • 고인숙
펴낸이 임 순 재

저자와의
협의하에
인지생략

펴낸곳 **한올출판사**
등록 제11-403호
121-849
주 소 서울시 마포구 성산동 133-3 한올빌딩 3층
전 화 (02)376-4298(대표)
팩 스 (02)302-8073
홈페이지 www.hanol.co.kr
e-메 일 hanol@hanol.co.kr
정 가 14,000원

□ ISBN 978-89-94948-91-1